Pauline Suett Barbieri

The Shirley Valentine Syndrome

In memory of my dear mother
who was forever
asking me as a child
if she was talking to the wall

First published in 2008
by Waterloo Press (Hove)
95 Wick Hall
Furze Hill
Hove BN3 1NG

Printed in Palatino 11pt by
One Digital
54 Hollingdean Road
East Sussex BN2 4AA

A CIP record for this book is available
from the British Library

ISBN 1-90731-36-0

By the Same Author

Pomes Pound the Page (*Oasis* Broadsheet, 2001)

Acknowledgements

Thanks go to the editors of the following journals in which some of these poems have previously appeared:

Acumen, Coffee House Poetry, Envoi, The Interpreter's House, Krax, Magma, The New Writer, Oasis, Orbis, Poetry Life, Poetry Monthly, PN Review, QueensPark Publishers, The Reader, Smiths Knoll, Staple, Tears in the Fence.

'Dancing with Mr. Armitage' was shortlisted for the Bridport Poetry Prize 2005. 'How can I do a Tango when I was brought up to Rock and Roll' received a Commendation in the Exeter Poetry Prize Competition 1998; 'Room 225 Hotel Rialto' received a commendation in the Exeter Poetry Prize Competition 1999; 'Passing the Buck' was placed in the *Poetry Life* Poetry Competition; 'For my father who was a tyrannosaurus when I was five' won 2nd Prize in the Wealdon Council Poetry Competition 2001; 'Manhattan Dream (1)' won First Prize in the Wealdon Council Poetry Competition 2002; 'Blue and White' is on display in Delft; 'Sestina for a City' was placed in East Street Poets Poetry Competition; 'Pomegranates at Delphi' appeared in Ver Poet's Prize Winning Anthology; 'Night Shift' won the Eastbourne Champion Women Poetry Postcard competition.

A novel, *Smoke and Gold* was shortlisted for the Cinamon Press Novel Awards. A short story was placed in the Writer's Bureau Short Story Competition, in Manchester. Barbieri was also shortlisted for 'Writer of the Year' by Writers' Inc., London.

Contents

IV: *The Dead End Kid*

V: *Save the Best to the Last*

I: *Camera Obscura*

MUSTARD

I am about two or three and my mother
is tying a stiff mustard–coloured bonnet
beneath my chin and it is too tight.
And I can't tell her.

We are standing on a bomb site,
perhaps having just left a shelter.
All I know is that I feel like
the ragman's horse,

wearing blinkers which shade my eyes
and reins which control my voice,
and neither of us knowing
the weight of the load we must carry.

RENOIR'S SWING

The space between leaves
is the most difficult to catch

                when a soft breeze blows.

The space between words
is the most difficult to let go

                when there's no echo.

Renoir's swing hangs low
in the afternoon, at ease

                with the spaces between

the leaves and the words.
Coupled love chains the day.

EPILEPSY

Chrome yellow clouds
Spinning, turning, maelstroming
Sunflowers stretching, retching
Lemons smelling of blond headed girls.
A chair, yes, I recognise
A simple, shiny, waiting
Chair, made of chrome yellow clouds
Spinning, turning
Sunflowers touching my cheeks
Lemons smelling of blond headed girls.
Burnished crows, miners and iconed widows.
Death waiting in the corner
Of a room I cannot reach. A room
In a yellow field, a chrome yellow chair,
In the corner of a room with an oblique floor
And a saffron painted bed with a scarlet cover.
A chrome yellow sky, a golden
Yellow chair in an oblique shaped
Room in a mustard coloured
House, spinning, turning
Maelstroming
Around an ochre stoned square
In the South of France
Under a spinning, smelting sun
Flowered sky.

STANDING WOMAN
Giacometti – 1948 Bronze

One
over–large
siamese
foot
holds
her
erect
She
stretching
gum–like
rises
skywards
female
stalagmite
The
air
around
her
divides
It
has
no
say
in
the
matter
Mauled
eyes
nose
and
gaping
mouth
beneath
beehived
skull
take
you
to her
Golgotha
You have no
say in the matter

ROOM 225 – *HOTEL RIALTO*

I found this poem in my room this morning
in the top left hand drawer
of the cabinet next to my bed.
It smelt of love and mothballs.

I lifted it up.
Some rotting Spanish adjectives fell away.
Carrying it gingerly to the open window
I shook it out over the wrought iron balcony.
Some purlised verbs dropped
onto the ledge below and stayed there.
A hungry Barcelonian pigeon
feathered cobalt blue
pecked at them, curiously.

The poem had a sort of hole
in the middle, perhaps a neck
which had, at one time, been darned
with black thread, caught up in the Twenties.

One knitted sleeve, red, was slightly
longer than the other.
The rib of alliteration had frayed
splayed, considerably.
Black and yellow crinkled letters hung limply
touched the ground, continued to run.

The receptionist said
that Miro had been born in that house.
Maybe this was something
his mother had made for him and
he could never bring himself to throw it away.

HOW CAN I DO A TANGO WHEN I WAS BROUGHT UP TO ROCK AND ROLL

My floor's well polished,
ready to explore
the brilliantined night.

Line, wind yourself
around my neglected waist,
curve my elbows
into the Tango's flight.
Follow the form
of a Latin lover's plight.

Adjectives flap against
the olive of your skin
Similes cling to the peaches
and cream of mine.

I bend, love's contortionist,
oiled by WD 40
and the smell of the Oleander
in your top suit pocket.

The band scrapes
the satinized notes off the floor,
lifts them high enough
for us to seize
and push into the space
between our hearts.

I lean into the night,
squeezing
your accordioned presence.
We writhe through
the mirrored ballroom
of our minds,
chase dreams
wedged
in highly polished shoes.

FELLINI'S 48 ½

Creeping under the half–shuttered
door of Belluci's tobacconists after
a free cigarette, Fellini takes a couple
of puffs which blow him into
an eight and a half world of sex.

Signora Belucci's mohair frontage
tickles his still smooth cheeks,
enhances his satyric curls,
offers him the chance of an early
trench–coated manhood.

Bottoms turn upside down,
jealous of bicycle seats;
the springs of love.
Smoke blares the lens
of his being, makes him screw up

his eyes until she fills the camera
which will eat his life,
suspend his desires,
keep him going back
to the tobacconist for more.

In a pizza parlour, fifty years later,
a pair of millefiori eyes bake
inside a moon brick oven.
Fellini desires a woman.
The tobacconist is closed.

Silicone breasts rise, still
to be proven. Fellini orders
the 'Grande'. Compliments the chef,
telling him 'La Dolce Vita
is in the hands of the beholder'.

THE GEOMETRY OF LINEN

I like ironing, the way the shirt gives itself
up to various angles. I find
the hypotenuse of the sleeves irresistible.
The square of the neck, promiscuous,
as it runs down to the tail, begging for steam.
Buttonholed cuffs spread out, unashamedly:
the dovetail of a swan looking for its reflection
in the surface of a mirror.
The firm shoulders ask nothing more than to sit
on the end of the board, square rooted,
padded, ready to support the daily load.

Switching the dial over to delicate,
a dress with flounces huffs and puffs about
like the sails of Ellen MacArthur's catamaran.
The iron starches the bodice, suspends it
around the world where it finds
wide angled breasts more than ready
to fill its warm backed curves.

Finally full blast into the equilateral
triangles set for a dinner table,
where the crimson-nailed fingertips
of some 'wannabe' celebrity
will unfold them like origami
and lay them across finely shaped knees
aching to nudge the knife-edged
trousers trembling alongside.

A KITCHEN SINK DRAMA

I hate doing the dishes but not tonight.
My new sponge is egg yolk yellow
and the soap is Italian pink. The colours
come together in a Renaissance bowl of water.

I sneak into the studio of Piero Della Francesca
to find the soldiers sleeping on duty.
But I can't be mad, they're tired like me.

I kiss the good looking one facing me.
Then, scraping some gold off his armour
I gild the rim of my bowl.

Placing a crimson shield behind the one
lying cramped against a stone, I ease
him gently down into its inviting curve.

Christ appears, disappointed, but his new golden halo
brightens his spirit. Lifting his robe,
the colour of my washing up liquid, he steps
out of the grave and goes off to town to astonish.

A third soldier now awake, sees his neglect of duty,
covers his eyes with shame. I sit down beside him
while Piero Della Francesca paints me in
with a yellow robe and pink halo, just to be different.

I whisper in his ear that God will forgive him
and everything will be alright
as Piero goes off to finish the dishes
just like he always did for his mother.

BLUE AND WHITE

Porcelain peeps out from between the canal ripples,
Vermeer is still asleep.
A girl brushes Sunday night into a tired gutter
as the bells of the Nieuwe Kerk toll
the beginning of the week.

'Leonidas' chocolate melts into
the coffee breath of the morning
as sleepy eyed workmen restore tiles
into the chessboard of life.

A mobile phone rings: a builder answers
but the bells of the Oude Kerk,
angry at the intrusion,
quiet his words.

Vermeer stirs
oil opens the brick red shutters
seduces Delft's early morning light.
Time to paint.

MES

Onbijt

It licks its early morning lips
at the golden waxed ball from Gouda,
powders itself into a Cat's creamier world.

Koffiedrinken

Blankaart's coffee rumours the day
whilst Claesz landscapes some starched linen,
clicks a wet silvered oyster open.

's Middags

Tired, lying disguised
on a tray full of fresh eels
from Rotterdam market. Resting,
breathing, after thirty years of slicing life.

's Avonds

Later a howl from Brouwer in a tavern
somewhere in Luilekkerland.
The knife stakes an ace of spades,
sawdust clings to its sweating handle,
blood stains the pudding.

s'Nachts

As I fall asleep, it slices a piece of the moon.
Reminds me of a lost lover,
sandwiches him between
my straight-laced sheets.

Mes – knife; *Onbijt* – breakfast; *Koffiedrinken* – coffee–break; *s'Middags* – lunch;
s'Avonds – dinner; *s'Nachts* – supper; Jacob Cats – 17th Cent. Dutch Emblematist;
Stephanus Blankaart – 17th Cent. Dutch physician; – prescribed coffee as a remedy
for mouldy joints and scurvy; Adriaen Brouwer (1605–1638) Flemish Painter.

PORTRAIT OF DOROTHY HODGKIN 1910–1994
by Maggie Hambling

Maggie gave you two pairs of hands
and an executive toy. There you play
at your desk, your knuckled fingers clicking
bones fossilised beneath your feathery hair.

Red, white and black balls chase
the molecules away on an old lady's
winter's day. The glass works hard,
jack–knifes a life, traces the spine of the room
where working models are displayed like blooms.

Maggie lights up another cigarette,
mixes paint, thinks about Miro and Calder,
how your kind of patterns knitted their work.

THE QUIET OF AGNES MARTIN
(North American Painter–1912–2004)

A luminous doyenne, framed
in a blank canvas, cut with graphite,
reveals the blood of a pioneer,
the sparkling waters of Saskatchewan.

Millet's postcard christens her teenage wall,
his 'Angelus' sending her on her way.
Krishnamurti offers her blossom,
D.T. Suzuki, an emptiness of mind.

The light of Taos, New Mexico
tapers her vision; twilight, snow,
the darkness creeping over her canvas
and the lonely pueblo of D.H. Lawrence.

This skeleton landscape stretches
canvas in her sailmaker's loft above
the bank–rolled vaults
of a steel–hearted Manhattan.

Newman, Reinhardt and Rothko sit watching
paint dry as she pulls away
from the crumbling kerb, leaving
everything behind, including the light.

Back in Taos, she starts to gesso
the mud bricked walls of her mind.
Washing white on white every morning
while the sun irons and starches her soul.

In the afternoons, she lounges around
with Agatha Christie and Poirot asking
what it's like to complicate. No television,
eight o' clock, it's off to bed.

Her life–sized canvas waits for dawn,
disciplined, holding a grid to realign the stars.
The newspaper on the mat, unopened,
in fifty years.

II: *GREECE*

POMEGRANATES AT DELPHI

The fruit seller's voice is urgent, dark,
trembling dried figs in the valley.
Tourists clamber up the black and white rocks,
desperate to escape the burning fleece of the sun.

'Ripe Fruit! Ripe Fruit!' His cries reach the summit.
Bouncing back they rattle the iron spokes of his cart.
Using a blade, forged around a slice of the new moon,
he cuts into the mound of glistening fruit.

Cool crystals cascade down
onto parched, crumbling paths.
The sky turns pink. People lift their heads,
reach for droplets the colour of unshed blood.

Down below, a teenage girl cups a handful,
then licks her ancient fingers clean.
The sun shadows a ravine, drops,
then waits at her feet.

She bends down and whispers, 'What do you want?'
The sun replies, 'You have eaten the truth'.

PERGAMUM

The Poplars, feather–like,
lose the last of their leaves
to the Aegean.

A shepherd pulls on the clothes
of his scattered animals.

The last of the cotton
refuses to be carried away
by an easterly wind.

And the Olive of Minerva stands
silent in its wisdom

As the tumbling ruins of Pergamum
wrap themselves
in the Winter parchment of time.

Pergamum – city in W. Asia Minor
where paper was invented.

FRAGMENT AT EDREMIT

I hear some word
of Sappho
as Lesbos
suds the sea returning
tidal flowers
restoring
poetry

HEPHAESTUS
(For Eduardo Paolozzi –
Chelsea Hospital – 12.12.2000)

Some days I wake with words
like a virus or bacteria
but I have no injection or antidote
and know they'll beat me down,
cling to me, bleed me like leeches,
creep behind my eyeballs, like glaucoma.

They'll get into my blood again,
stream to places I've never been
if I let them. But I'm afraid
they may find something I don't know about,
don't recognize, can't handle
or a place not strong enough
to carry off the fight.

They keep pushing medicine back
up my piping throat.
My temperature drops to below zero,
keeps the doctors worried,
scurrying from screens, looking for
healing stuff. But these words are tough,
don't hang about the outer edges, dig deep,
get inside the shadow of the heart,
the lace canticles of the lungs.

They embroider the brain.
That's where it all starts.
They clog up the vessels,
then form an army to batter
down the doors of the heart.
At the moment they're struggling,
can't get up the lichen covered rampart
but they'll try again. After dark.

GALLIPOLI

As the quiet and unassuming
Dardenelles carries me from
the East to the West
like an old man who has seen it all

I sit sandwiched between
two old ladies, a Mongol and a Turk
– both smiling.

And as I think of Byron
and his swim from shore to shore
my mind joins the golden fleece
above the fields of war.

Then I recall my own soldier father,
and realize, while chewing a pretzel
in freedom, that old soldiers never die
they ebb and flow each day.

III: *THE HEART IS WHERE THE HOME IS*

THE DUET

The piano has no keys
As the pianist starts to play.
He sees a landscape of flesh
Its hills lead him astray.

But the landscape has no sky
As the dreamer drifts to a beat.
She sees a keyboard of silk
Which scores her ivory feet.

So he plays a tune with no fingers
And she dreams a dream with no feet.
He ties her with black and white ribbons
As she pumps the piano asleep.

LINGERIE

Last night
I slept in a metaphor.
It was silk, vermilion.
It came in a brown cardboard box
with tissue surrounds
flecked with gold.
It was my exact size.
It clung to me
with midnight hands,
still wet,
covered with droplets,
eked
from the waters
of the netherworld

SESTINA FOR A CITY

I have left but am still leaving this city.
Its charcoal slate slides close to winter
recycles the home of my mother.
I lean across the Mersey's sleeve, touch
a sandy cuff running along New Brighton's skin,
sound the river, skim the city's fallen.

This Liver bird flies, has never fallen
though chased through caverns. The city
refuses to crease the family's skin,
hides it in Sefton Park's greenhouse, where winter
fingers the glass, recalls the Midas touch.
It leafs my eyes to silver, transmutes my mother

to gold, freezes the baseness of life. Mother,
you call, often in the dreams of the fallen.
I clasp your hand, fill my bucket, touch
the nearest star, sprinkle it onto this city,
where the blackout of an eyeless winter
find Everton Brow, folds it within its skin.

Back home, tackling the freckled, flashing skin
of my father, a jousting ever present mother,
is ready to fight to earn the only fruit of Winter.
I hide it the basket of the fallen
until Summer comes again to this city
and the sun returns with my mother's touch.

The cathedrals clap on the hill. Keep God in touch.
While a cobbled edge rattles Anfield's skin,
crumbles, clashes, cymbals a playful city.
But I look for a substitute for a mother,
turning away from the empty bench of the fallen,
shaking the bare trees, courting a makeshift Winter.

One where the landing stage floats free. This winter
acknowledges a shift in time. Ferries touch,
feel their way, screeching, peeling tyres. Fallen
from the Pier Head, their rubberised skin
saving the life of the river god. A sailor's mother
haunting the docks, catches his cry for the city.

I must wait until it stops digging under my skin,
to catch the tug boat puffing out to join my mother,
who has left but is still leaving this city.

NAMES TO CONJURE WITH

'Farinelli, Barbieri' – Is that the only thing
we have in common – family names
ending in an Italian eye?
But this one is not mine.
It was a gift, thirty years ago,
from an Italian lover.
It aprons another me, a daughter
caught in a butcher's chain.

But look! See how we are both scarred,
ligatures about us, straining,
gasping, cleaving the air.
But your voice manages to escape
with an empyrean beauty,
dissolving Philip's melancholia
every Spanish night, over ten years.

Whilst mine sits echoing beneath
a fifty year old basin hairstyle.
Just another singing 'Suett' on the shelf.
Ridicule, bullying, flickering resentment
at a father's name, held steaming.
A string drawn tightly around
a boned and filleted smile.

And still, I look for a song, now outside
Covent Garden, recalling an ancestor, Theophilus.
Too nervous, or sick perhaps, for his debut
as Samson, at that house in eighteen hundred.
His voice, the century's phantom.

Whilst an old handed understudy,
'Dicky', his father, celebrated
fool and jester raises the curtain
to mad King George, bows
and mixes the pudding
of our forever butchered lives.

Farinelli (real name Carlo Broschi) 1705–1782 Italian singer
Richard 'Dicky' Suett 1755–1805 Shakespearean clown/singer/actor/
composer
Theophilus Suett 1780 – ? Singer/musician/actor

A ROSE
For Bukowski

I wonder.
Do I need face
replacement
therapy
or perhaps
lip–suction
technique
on my brain.

I don't think so.
All I really need,
I suppose,
is a rose sometimes.
Preferably from a man
with no name
and a big nose.

OTHELLO

Our house was a Bassett house,
sooty walls, whitewashed yard and pink candy
striped curtains I used to twist in my bedroom.

In the school holidays I'd look up, dry–mouthed, watching
the barley sugar sun licking the tarmac'd shed of the roof
where I lay sunbathing with black and white cats.

Winters, the snow came in
balls, blue like the edge of the nebula, I now see
expanding on my wide–screen television.
Hundreds and thousands of sugar–coated particles

nudging the pink coconut one around
like my mother's tired powder puff
coating her soft–centred skin.

And in the middle, my favourite, the stub of liquorice.
Hard and chewy, making my mouth water
like the black man who came on frosty Sunday mornings
and sang in the middle of the street.

LARD

It was as if Mathew Street was about to cave in
when the first note fell off the back of a lorry
with no wing mirrors to see where it had come from.

Soot encrusted walls coughed up the din.
Rats came out of cellars, tails in the air, listening to the music.
The Mersey was bobbing up and down on her toes.

Warehouses grabbed hold of the sounds,
stuffed them inside giant cartons of lard
newly arrived and repackaged from America.

Later, the lard would pan chips in the back kitchen
and the songs would fry in a fat so hot,
you couldn't stand near the stove.

BOLT

Being a girl I don't know that
much about screws but the one
in my pocket makes me feel good
as if my world can't fall apart. As
I run my warm fingertips
over the cool
thread, I can
imagine using
it, slotting it in
to a joint. In
fact I think it
is a bolt with
two nuts, one
at each end but only one
is free. Perhaps
this is what
they call a
wing. My life
was like that.
Open ended.
Waiting for
some angel to come along
who knew all
about a mortise
and tenon.
It also has two
washers, loose
wobbly, unsure
which way to
turn.Like our
wedding rings during the
ceremony. Luckily you had
the right kind of spanner.
Knew how to drive in your
love so that there was no
way I could turn
back without
destroying
the thread

SELF PORTRAIT

A nice cut, straight off her father's block,
with cheeks full and only slightly veined.
Hazel eyes borrowed from a mother
still denying their age. Here and there,
moles and warts of wasted wisdom.

The look of one who's lampooned life.
The mouth's Cupid's, perfect in its bow,
timed, ready to shoot the last laugh.
The forehead pouched, heavy with jokes.

This is not in oils, acrylic or water
but shuttered on a dull grey day
to record the variations of shade,
to be found in a century's time
alongside a small poem
written on the inside of her left hand.

WIMBLEDON 2005

The defending champion appears on the centre court
where the gold ringed net catches my eyes.
I struggle in the grassy waters of a final game,
anxious to escape thirty year old dust.

His deeply carved eye sockets
remind me of yours on the nights you returned
from a shift in the morgue, exhausted
by your work in cancer research.

Still trapped in the heat of what you looked like,
the camera zooms into his full lips, stolen
from Cupid, longing to be kissed.
I bob along the baseline after the air in his gold trainers.

The right kind of headband ticks his black lacquered hair,
parts it above the smouldering whites of his eyes.
His double racquet case, masking a guitar,
swings into 'Young Girl'. Told to run, she melts into the sun.

Wondering how you could let your doppelganger take over
in a love match where rain stopped play in Philadelphia,
I don't have the guts for another tie breaker.
I flick the channel, hit 'Live 8', again try to make love, history.

BROTHER

He had curls. Tight, like those liquorice whirls
which always got stuck on the inside of the jar.
And not just a couple but more than you could squeeze
into one of those giant jars in Mrs. Mangan's sweetshop.

And me with straight hair, the colour of Hovis
and as sad as the parlour curtains at a funeral.

In the kitchen, plonked under an egg speckled basin,
I would be given a haircut. Holding onto my earlobes,
my blood congealed into black puddings
as snippets fell around his feet dangling out of the pram.

And him looking up under the basin, smiling,
all the while licking a scarlet lollipop.

THE CALLER

Can you imagine a street,
a cul-de-sac
with brick walls the colour of soot.
And pavements scrubbed
to resemble the powdered
bottom of a baby.
The tarmac'd middle,
a stick of liquorice
stretching to the moon.

Then imagine
the arrival of an American car
in the fifties, its bumpers touching
both sides of the street.
Marshmallow-coloured,
metal–trimmed, mirrors caught
in the face of a coal mine.

And the interior –
Imagine seats
the colour of Betty Grable's lips,
as curvaceous as Jane Russell's hips
and me waiting as an eleven year old,
for the movie to start.

Can you imagine
seeing the car parked
outside number thirty seven,
where my friend Patsy, a teenager,
lived, with eyes glistening like a snowman's
and a mass of ebony curls
tighter than my father's drill.

Then imagine
the driver of the car, with skin the colour
of coconut oil and jewelry chaining
his shot-silk suit,

laughing so loud it echoed
back home in Chicago.

I could hardly imagine
what they did in the afternoons
behind her aunt's aspidistra
while she was out shopping.

FOR MY FATHER WHO WAS A TYRANNOSAURUS
WHEN I WAS FIVE

If Hitler had of met my dad, he would have polished his boots.
He would have stood at the end of the lobby
unable to lift his arms above his waist.

If Hitler had of met him, there wouldn't have been a war.
He would have stayed for tea on Sunday
with cakes, jellies and scrubbed hands.

If Hitler had heard my dad romancing the Roman Catlicks,
after he'd been converted, he would have sold his tanks.

If Hitler had come to our house, he would have seen a fort
built by my dad. Green, sawdusted, precision-crusted in every
joint,
he could have played with it and gone home happy.

If Hitler had of met him, he would have wanted to play for Liver-
pool
and my dad would have talked to Shankley.

If Hitler had of met my dad, he would have bought a ferry-boat
and sailed back to Berlin with a load of chip-butties.

If Hitler had of met him, the Gerries would have wanted to twin
with Liverpool and my dad would have kept them waiting.

If Hitler had of met my dad, even at fifty,
he still would have done what he was told.

Oh! I forgot he did.

THE KITCHEN

Sometimes I feel incredibly sad,
my heart, a colander letting go
of white blossoms.

Or a Spanish guitar
in an Autumn garden,
its notes stretching,
golden bindweed
around a mother's memory.

Until it finally unribbons
into a face by Dali.
My mother watching
through timeless spaces,
rattling the pots and pans,

singing.

HUSBAND

Sometimes when I think of you,
I see you as a plough
pushing your way through
a landscape of colour.

At other times, you are
just a furrow in a field,
letting oil and colour shape
you, at will.

Occasionally I see you as a ball
of energy hitting the canvas,
a diffracted laser beam
splitting atoms of colour.

Rarely I see you, only as a shadow,
when all energy has been zapped,
your spirit trapped inside a giant canvas
which hangs, strangely quiet, on our walls.

LUMBER

The tree, looking back at itself, gnarled
    into a monkey puzzle. A ten year old
        chimp of a nephew straddled the canopy.

Nibbling at the sweetest branch, his own,
    he started to count rings; a homework task
      for the Spring holiday.

Palming some lower branches, he studied
    the undergrowth on our side. His mother
      my sister, our father, our great baboon
         of a grandfather swinging through time

back to seventeen fifty and a missing link
    with George the Third. Earlier, the Doomsday Book
      revealed a lone family, our name falling

steadily through the seasons. Between the two,
    an offshoot into Scotland, a falcon
      on our mother's side, soaring

into the Macpherson clan. My sister married
    a foreigner. A dark eyed seducer from the East,
      arriving with the moon and the stars
        in a hand made wicker basket. His mother

came from the same branch as his father,
    along with the genetic fault. Their grandson now perched
      on a risky branch, looked earnestly at me,

his tremble, the family's crest. 'Daddy told me last night that
    his grandfather had seven wives'. In one swing,
      he felled my tree into a forest of sand.

SUPPER

Einstein's brain would probably have looked quite boring
on a butcher's counter. It being described
as a darker shade of grey. Not that it matters,
all the rest being a lighter shade of pale. Or pink.

It had wide lobes with enough material
to keep the next generation thinking a long time.
I asked Doctor Thomas whether it would stay fresh.
Was informed that with that kind of mental activity
it had probably never died. Although it did stink.

I often thought about brains as a child,
especially as they had them on Saturday night
after the pub, if the chip shop had run out of pig's feet.
I'd never heard of science until I went to the movies
and saw *Frankenstein*. He had no brain.

T.L.F.L.
(Teaching Love as a foreign language)

Students, as I remember, were always
snotty nosed brats just hanging around,
waiting for our convent schoolgirl knickers
to fall down. How come, when I advertised
my services, some thirty years later,
the boys turned out to be all over
twenty one, almost rich, with noses like
                          Michaelangelo.

Now as a straight laced English girl I knew
that I'd have no trouble giving language
lessons, handing out lines, keeping them in.
But somebody had broken the bell.

I noticed pupils sliding down into the corner
of olive skinned eyes. Latin blood leaning over
desks while sensual foreign accents blew
the last of the chalk off the board. Leonardo curls
took on that fleshy pink tinge of a sublime
Tuscan sunset and lips began to pout
and bow like those kissing the ceiling
                          in the Vatican.

I stood in my favourite Fair isle
jumper and brown leather lace-ups,
wondering which one of them
would tell me the Italian word for 'No'.

IV: *THE DEAD END KID*

FATTY ARBUCKLE WELCOMES ME TO THE USA

The Immigration officer was bigger than the 747 I had just landed in.
He wore his badges like he had made them himself

out of the sun. So bright, my mother was probably
admiring them back home in Liverpool.

His custom made gun, slinging on his belt, looked louder
than the one fired, at one o'clock, over the Mersey.

I stood in front of him, a lone teenager with a cardboard suitcase.
A mote of uranium inside a single bullet, heading for a game
        of roulette.

Arriving at the barrier in Kennedy Airport in the Spring of '65
it was as if he'd brought the whole of Hollywood to greet me

but the only thing that was showing was a Dead End Kid.

'BUT ALL THE FUN'S IN HOW YOU SAY IT'
– Robert Frost

I've just been reading a piece of writing
about a mountain in America
by this fellow, or fella, depends whether
you're out of the country or the city.

He writes about living in the country
which almost makes me cry. I can't imagine
what that is like, being a city girl.

He talked about this mountain being a
black shadow he could lean on with
houses lying around the bottom like
boulders broken off the upper cliffs. And

I remembered leaning on something like
that as a girl. The giant black waterworks
with houses dotted about it like old
raindrops or tarmac blisters waiting to plop.

He talked about wandering around looking
for a path to the summit and he meets
a man with white faced oxen who tells him

the way. I thought about how you could reach
the top of the waterworks and the light
and what kind of men built it. I wandered

alone, around the charcoal railings, met
a man with a white face and a raincoat.
It wasn't raining but he was strangely
intent on showing me how water works.

THE MAN WHO WAS JEALOUS OF
MARIANNE MOORE'S HATS

Swore often. Wore a never wanted to roam hat
Lived alone. Had a sit by the fire hat with a singed rim
A glow from within cap

Sometimes he longed for a fox hat
An Artic pair of socks hat
King pinned with penguins, black and white sequinned
A wake me up to the midnight sun cap

Once he dreamed her dragon hat
A drag on and off hat
A slip over the tongue hat, forked with flaming envy
The mind's an enchanted thinking cap

His Saturday nights wanted her tiger hat
Piping hot behind striped breasts and bottoms hat
Disco stomping, mind goes romping
A take the girls for a riding cap

He once saw her wearing a pangolin hat
As shiny as a mandolin
A throw a man a hand grenade cap

She had a hard on-site hat
Difficult to digest
Of no assistance to a pass the test cap

He had heard rumours about a rhino horn hat
A Viagra silk lined bowler
A stay up all night in the bed cap

Sometimes she wore a divine hat
Nothing mundane about it
A drive you literary insane cap

Occasionally, she wore
her loss can never alter Socrates' tranquillity hat
But on off days, it seemed more of a hemlocked cap

One day in New York, she sent for him
Said she needed a keep down the rats' hat
His aunt's Second World War hat
The godmother to this rat with an attitude hat

FORD MALIBU

It was there for more than thirty years,
at the back of the drawer.
A tag. Scratched plastic, said
'Trenton' and something else.
Worn out. Probably 'New Jersey'.
Its car was yellow on the outside.
Black interior.

It held us secure as a leather
glove belonging to the Mafia. Held us
locked in and down that street in
New York. That night at midnight
at the end of your shift. Not far
from the Chinese restaurant where
Hopper would sit on a wooden bench
with noodles. Opposite me
and my friend, wearing hats. Mine
was an emerald green Stetson with
a black tie. And hers? I can't remember.

But I remember being locked in
your yellow car in that dark street
and the gang of rats with shiny coats
and bright chalky eyes ready
to blackboard death, who had followed you
from the morgue, circled your car,
looking for scraps.

Then the pathologist in you
opened the door to death, in defiance.
Life, the only weapon in your hands
challenging silver knives
slashing windows, sparking like those
the old man sharpened on his wheel
in our street, on Sundays. And their teeth
jagging the night, snarling, hissing
at your Hollywood bravado.

The car and me turning
a lighter shade of pale beneath
the projectionist's faltering lamp.
My screams held you back.
I was not ready to lose you.
You pulled away from the kerb
into another shot but
nobody yelled 'Cut!'

HOTEL TROPICANA – LAS VEGAS

where the waiter wants to be
the newly implanted breasts
of the platinum blonde, standing
in front of the fruit machine
which has just hit three lemons.
He also fancies flicking the wrist
of the red headed dealer from Delaware
who's caressing the green backed table, number fifteen.
At a pinch, he could be the fat guy who can't get
his legs around the carved cornice
of the brunette who serves ice blue cocktails
in the booth at the corner.

He sighs, straightens his thighs, makes
a bee line for the rollers on a high.

He used to be a red chip in the hands of the croupier
whose dress keeps getting pleated by
the overworked air conditioning in the corner.
Tonight, though, he's decided to be the card
in the slot of the lock of room seventeen,
where the wife of the fat millionaire at table two
sits alone, drinking, bored out of her
rotating fruit balled eyes, waiting
for the knickerbocker glory
which is slowly melting on the tray
in front of his dark hairy throat.

147 EAST 69TH STREET
for Taya Thurman

The night, exhausted, takes the subway
downtown to Grand Central. Changes,
becomes first light.
Undressed yellow knocks at the door,
opens to a white buttercup.
Rothko takes the flower, powders it
down onto his laid back palette.
Crushes sunshine into his egg yolked day.

Madison Avenue succumbs to glistening corn,
pops out to watch the dollar starting to play.
It was one of your better days,
the day the Deli man called
with foot high, hot pastrami, sizzling
French mustard and Perugino Baci.
Your purples, singed siennas and dark
chocolate still slept under the stairs.

East Sixty Ninth Street was curdling Manhattan
through your early morning colours.
Pimps smelt you burning the pancakes.
Police crawled along scrambled pavements.
The Mafia ordered lemon silk suits.
The Statue of Liberty bent over Central Park,
cleaned your brushes with turps.

MANHATTAN DREAM (1)

I remember he said, '42nd Street,
outside Grand Central'.
The reason I remember
was because I thought he,
Rod Stewart, was about to sing it
there and then, on the phone.

I could even see him
wearing a lemon meringue suit
in crease resistant satin.
It had risen in exactly the right places.
Just like it should in an oven.

I went to meet him after getting
an expensive makeover at Macey's
and waited until Wednesday.
That was around six on Saturday night.
Later, I heard he used another entrance
to avoid the crowds. And me too?
Or did I remember him saying,
'....the side entrance...'?

MANHATTAN DREAM (2)

He didn't tell me he was coming to take me out
but when I woke up, I had a tan.
I'd been to St.Moritz for the weekend with Omar Sharif.

His eyes were frosted, like I remembered in the films,
and when he kissed me they melted.
My pillow was still wet when I woke up.

MANHATTAN DREAM (3)

My bath was sort of square, like an old gunslinger's
in white enamel with curved edges.
Copper bottomed, I had a dream in it.
I fell out of a hole in a 747,
landed outside a bar on Madison Avenue.

I got up, dusted myself down, then walked down the middle
coming face to face with a cop on traffic duty.
'That plane! That plane!' I screamed 'is going to crash!'
Dragon's flames shot out of the tail. Its barrel still smoking.
'No Ma'am, don't worry, it aint!' He reassured me.

Nervously due to fly home the next morning,
I called the airline. Was I travelling on a 747?
'No, a smaller one. Would you like a transfer
to the big one flying later in the day?'
'No thank you,' I said, holstering the phone.

Home safe and sound but missing my cowboy bath
and donuts a few days later, I went down to the bakers,
then onto the newsagents to get a copy of 'U.S.A. Today.'
It was dated the day after I left with a headline, '747 aborts takeoff,
lands on runway with tail on fire. J.F.K. confirms no casualties'.

TO THE EDGE WITH WALLACE STEVENS

He takes me to the edge.
And no further.

He offers me a flower
from which he has rinsed the perfume.

He guides me back
along the tramlines of childhood,

to the woods where even the cuckoo
has sold him his song.

He slides his arm under mine
whispers the unsayable,

offers me colours, gifts,
whipped off the washing line of the gods.

He goes ahead. I follow him
hanging, bat–like,

I strain to catch the dandelion
caught in the charcoal crevice

of his ever plummeting abyss.

CALIFORNIA RED – £3.99

Sony's Megabass plays Beethoven
as canyons carve their way into sleepy ears,
dust red powder onto tired cheeks.
I catch the violin, hear the piano
pouring over wet rocks.
Wine trickles down the bottle, runs
into the blue of the label.
The violin strains, stretches like wet tights
on the line after a hard day. It squeezes
my thoughts until the strings cauterise my lungs,
refusing to let me go until the fat lady has sung.

The shuttle flies above, pregnant
with seven astronauts in a space orchestra.
Floating to the sounds of the earth;
plastic cups crackle nervously,
somebody coughs in the control room.
They take it into their dancing chamber,
let it exhale into the spaceless night.

The music, jealous, nudges in between
the relaxing metal of the shuttle's ribs.
Beethoven reaches out of an ebony air,
listens to a soundless world, takes stars,
pins them onto the velvet score of my mind.

Together we join the space crew, float
into the station where music spills out
as mercury, finds the astronauts, sends
their thoughts back to earth.

I step into high heeled shoes with needled toes,
feel the silk of a whirling tango'd life,
hear the whisper of women somewhere
on a dark street in Brazil, peeling the scarlet
of their dresses smouldering around
the cast off engine of the shuttle,

which has just fallen somewhere
near a jealous heart.

THE ART OF LOSING

Catch the night bus from Philly.
Sleep 'til the tunnel pushes you outside.
Manhattan splashes your lashes with glitter,
takes your tears to the top of the Empire State,
hangs them out to dry.

Madison Square Garden unbandages your heart,
takes the seconds out of your corner,
invites you to take on someone else.

The dance hall on Forty Second polishes its brass.
The orchestra has heard you're back in town.
The Lorelei on Eighty Sixth Street has already started
pickling the midnight cabbage and the museum
of Modern Art is hanging out Sunday.

Ride up to Harlem, don't stop for a red.
Listen to Billy on the radio.
Open a fire hydrant. Refuse to play dead.

Back down to Wall Street with a hole
as big as your heart. Ground Zero waits for lovers,
where they've turned losing into a fine art.

THE FAT LADY'S SONG

Some clown has let go of the balloons.
The safety net is caught on the tip of the moon.
Tightrope walkers cable the sky, turn up the sun.

Lions pretend to be sleeping in a cage
with a single bar, where the Master of Ceremonies
orders a cocktail, a 'Camel's Hump'

to carry him across a desert
of out–of–date custard pies
and environmental officers' interactive cries.

The bears prefer to go down
to the woods, stop off at Macdonald's,
take Ronald for a picnic.

Red and yellow acrobats no longer know how to bend,
they ride white elephants like your flexible friend,
only flipping over to take the cash and dash.

The horses prefer the easy going
in Ladbrooks. Refuse to entertain
a flaming powder–kegged dance.

String-vested rope boys still look up
for Gina Lollabrigida, are tired of stretching
a star–spangled canvas for the finale

where Pierrot has lost the collar without a dog,
wears ready–made tears from Poundland,
pays the orchestra to download life.

PINOCCHIO'S DREAM

I noticed that when I began to write fiction
my nose started getting longer.
When it first happened, I got a shock
but now it doesn't bother me anymore.
But it keeps knocking up against the page,
sometimes smudges the words.
They're all lies of course. Now I tell them
all the time. There was no point
in telling the truth. Who was interested?
As soon as I mentioned the word,
poetry, people would scarper. Anyway,
what is poetry? Only words to keep
my nose in place. I thought a long nose
might help but it didn't. You see, I discovered
I didn't write poetry, it wrote me.
I used to smell it coming. It came in wafts.
Not like this chunk of a nose
which appears every time I write. It's ugly
but I don't have the money for plastic surgery.
Apparently, you can have a kind of Peter Pan
nose that never changes, despite
how many lies you tell. Even you
believe you're telling the truth.
But this kind of operation is only carried out
in a place called Never Never Land,
which is so difficult to get into, you never can.
Every day I hope some brilliant carver
will come along and chisel my nose to a fine
silverpoint, ready to etch truth and fiction
into a very special kind of story
that will be read forever and ever.

PASSING THE BUCK

Age is contagious. Once you have silver hair
and a bus pass, nobody stops to speak to you.
Especially nobody like you – a Greek God – I tell myself
as you sit down opposite me in the college café.
Yet you offer me a smile, your name,
a conversation; some nectar of life.

I recall 'Philly' forty years ago and the bum
who came into a bar with no money. I bought him a drink.
He said his name was Buk, wrote poems to pass the time,
liked Borodin to wash down his wine.
His nose was three times as big as yours.
His poems a thousand times bigger than mine.

A 'Crucifix in a Deathhand' grabbed me in a junk shop
a while ago. His first collection put together
by himself whilst plastered in New Orleans;
the pages mixed up with whisky and rye.
And a signature in pink ink hidden inside the back cover;
his kiss waiting for me. The Internet says it's priceless.

A month later I'm back near the Common Room
I recognise your voice. You're talking to a fellow student.
Your boss has vanished, no wages for a week, no money for food.
Your elegant cheekbones now look haggard,
the cave in your chest belongs to an El Greco or a Giacometti.
Catching my eye, you come over and sit down.

I keep trying to remember your name
and still you smile even though you starve.
Then suddenly you say mine.
I flip open my bag and take out the twenty pound note
I just got for the last poem I managed to get published.
'Here! Get yourself something to eat.'

A student, listening nearby, says 'That's sweet of you',
his gentle language almost condescending age.
Before darting outside to get some food,
you kiss my cheek. 'Thank you', you say and are gone.
I'd like to see you again because I gave you the note
not because you were hungry but because you had no name.

PUTTING ON FRANK O'HARA'S BOXER SHORTS

Sorry Frank! But your book remained
closed while your dark part was open.
I bought your 'Selected', stashing it
inside the lining of my old raincoat.

Back home, I hid it under an encyclopedia
for fear my Dutch Puritan husband
would spot the cover, wonder how I could justify
Larry River's explicit collage as art.

T.R. Yoseloff – 1998, a signature inside,
the previous owner with a mileage
of five hundred thumbprints on the poetometer,
was no doubt more tuned in to your kind of engine.

But now, after two months on the shelf, I want to take
a bigger bite. Peeling off a strip of black, sticky
electrical tape, I cut out a nice pair of boxer shorts
and place them strategically over your more than gay part.

The fabric adamantly clings, then wrinkles,
exactly how you would have wanted it to,
standing in front of a nice
respectable convent girl like me.

V: *SAVE THE BEST TO THE LAST*

HIDE AND RECYCLE

1900AD
A cow lounges in a field like an old settee.

2000AD
An old settee in a field lounges like a cow.

THE NIGHT I REALIZED GOD WAS A VACUUM CLEANER

According to your cosmologists
when one of our neighbours in Andromeda
is getting ready to go out for the night,
they sometimes let dandruff fall
onto our rubbing shoulders
but as we're both travelling pretty fast,
half a million miles an hour,
most of it gets blasted out of sight.
But some, determined, hangs on tight.

That's when the vacuum cleaner comes out.

If he misses a bit, which can happen
even to God, it cottons on to a quasar;
sort of gigantic haloes spinning faster
than last week's washing in the launderette.
Floss comes off these things like candy,
condenses on the outer edge of supersoft clouds
and, if they happen to be in the wrong place
and God's short of time, these left-over
stars find themselves on a black-holed line.

That's why a vacuum cleaner went through my mind.

The thirty six sided, silver-plated mirror
astronomers managed to solder together
was just about strong enough to catch me,
last night, on my way out. I'd just been created.
Standing a bit surprised at the edge of a white hole
tucked into a fold of the Milky Way, I saw them,
the 'Nukers'. Black hole explorers way out
past Andromeda, obviously feeling the strain.

Suddenly the vacuum cleaner was switched off.

Then I saw her, the lady on last night's 'Horizon'.
The one with dark hair and glasses.
Of course, at that moment, I don't think she could see God.
He was around the back, emptying some ashes.
But I had just been stirred and shaken out of his dust bag.
Given some air. She must have seen me
on her screen, so fresh and sparkling, 'Godsware'.

That's when I realized God was a vacuum cleaner.

I know it's not easy to believe God
is a vacuum cleaner especially as, next year,
I hear they're bringing out a silent model;
a computerised version which emits perfume.
I know you won't believe it but he's already okay'd it.
Said he needed a bit more peace and quiet
for doing other things, like bending rainbows,
reading comets, visiting relatives,
the good ones, measuring them for haloes.

THE FINAL

Someone said he was wearing the number 10 shirt.
One thing, he knew how to score goals,
being the culmination of the Blessed Trinity:
Gerard, Crouch and Owen.
Every time he tackled someone, the kop went quiet
but he was never one for showboating,
he just returned the goals to heaven.
Every time he nutmegged Rooney, he faced the devil
who was in goal with three legs.
But even the ref was friendly, shying a red card,
giving him only three 'Our Fathers' and a 'Glory Be'
for one hell of a foul.

Half time it was a draw. A priest appeared
with crates of lager and packets of crisps.
The 'Ref' blew his whistle.
The players dashed down to the changing rooms,
whispered desperate confessions into steel lockers.

The whistle brought them back on again
to the Kop's chant of The Kyrie.
He ran out in front wearing his golden boots
The kop went wild as he performed a captain's blessing.
A rough match; they were down to seven men,
two minutes before the final whistle. They held
their breath as he flicked the ball inside a halo
but the devil kicked his ankle, buckled his knee.
A cry for penalty was heard. Acknowledged in limbo time.
He placed the ball on the spot,
hung his head, winked at the goalie,
watched him saying his prayers.

'BOYS IS NASTY...MIGHT AS WELL
..........ASK WIMEN..........'
(Mr. Wheezely – from 'The Outing' by Dylan Thomas)

A boy dances to a different tune
as the eleven–a–side waltz towards goals
where banknotes are tucked into a net
like the cleavage of a nightclub dancer.

The roar of the trainer moves hips faster
than her roving eyes on Sunday morning in the park.
Her honey coud be yours
as you fly in your black and yellow kit.

Joining a swarm of killer bees
you ardently follow the dance of the queen
who flies backwards and forwards
striping honeycombed lines.

The smell of her greasepaint draws you,
sends you buzzing past a yellow,
skirting around a red into a lone dance
where the crowd demands your sting.

SERIOUS INTENT

What do they look like, these poets of serious intent.
Do they wear blue stockings which wrinkle a literary bent.

Perhaps they have iambic feet which causes them to strut
or do they just wobble a bit on a catalectic foot.

Are they set in concrete, cracking poems throughout the land
or do they sport a trochee and beat the prosey band.

Do they suffer from lineation and take breaks at every chance
even claiming slight amnesia to indulge in consonance.

Perhaps they eat enjambent butties and wash in dactyl bowls,
say it all in a monometer while tutors unfurl scrolls.

Can they cook a delicacy of literary words anew
then sit around a poetic urn and serve an empiric stew.

Dare they voice a villanelle or find the going tough
leaving them to Master Dylan who seamed them off his cuff.

Can they take an octave and knock it for a six
then hand around an allegory with a hyperbolic fix.

Would they risk a roundel and come back from where they've been
seeking songs before sunrise with an Atalantan beam.

Perhaps they have an accent which causes anapaest
with blank looks from foreign scribes whose seriousness is best.

And who will offer a paradox of serious intent –
All poets are ageing liars of a somewhat truthful bent.

I HATE BUYING FRENCH BREAD

I do it furtively as if clad in an extra large
raincoat because it always sticks out of the bag
like something you can only buy in Soho.

If it's extra long, I usually fold it in two
but it flaps against the plastic
like some disgruntled fly–trap.

Other times the crust peels off.
Especially on the ones I have
to carry onto a train.

A one–track mind pursues
visions of bastard buns
overdone in some waiting oven.

But sometime in France, early morning,
I buy a French loaf and suddenly become
wrapped in pink and white gingham

with a blond pony–tail, swaggering
my way back to my lover.
Whistling at the thought

of my freshly–baked goods.
The breeze blowing a pink satin
ribbon in my soft maiden hair.

A THEORY OF RELATIVITY

He could have been anyone of us,
going into number eleven, with big hair and no socks.
Curious to see if anyone would turn up. The curtains drawn,
as mysterious as the formula up his chalky sleeve.

Every Tuesday, the seance called us
like landscaped figures in the unequal equation of life.
Space invaded time at his command.
He sat, his knees knocking under Mrs. Katzenellenbogen's
table from the sea. Driftwood longing to be free.

Once the light was out and the candles lit,
the curtain to the back kitchen would start rippling.
He said it was the expansion of the universe
but Mrs. Katzenellenbogen said it was only
the silent ones passing through.

One time he was busy calculating the shifting table
when the candle set fire to his curls.
The burn out was expected. Impressive. They sizzled

under his scribbling hands as he caught the light,
the mass and the undeniable weight of relatives
generating energy under the missing table.

Smoke swirled around his bushy moustache.
He sat like an old, mellow but excited walrus.
'Does the inertia of a body depend on its energy content?'
He asked Mrs. Slater from number fifty two

who couldn't wait to get into the kitchen
and start peeling an atom with him.
But she had to. He had no equation; $E=MC2$
having been singed out of all recognition from the tablecloth.

He refused to budge. He was determined to gain proof.
Proof of the afterworld. He would capture it, throw a laser around it.
He was happy being part of the particles, knowing
there was always an uncertainty principle out there.
Somewhere. She could turn up any night.

Mrs. Katzenellenbogen had asked him often enough
not to come. His musings disturbed the spirits.
Especially since he told Mrs. Brown from number five
'I cannot believe God plays dice with the cosmos'.

Mrs. Brown was flummoxed. She had only just lost
Mr. Brown and she was not a gambling woman.
But he wanted to comfort her. Prove something.
That Mr. Brown's relativity was still very close. Perhaps.

He brought out his photon album which he opened
at the speed of light. Mrs. Brown had hardly time
to say hello to Mr. Brown before he was again
reduced to a polarised sight.

Out of the blue. Out of the smoke.
Induced by the working of his calculating mind,
Mileva and Elsa parted the uncertainty curtain
and proved that love was thicker than tea leaves.

He was astounded. Wanted both of them
behind the curtain. But there already, shrouded in blue velvet,
waited Betty and Margarette, who had elbowed their way
into the seance past Elsa and Estella.

There were so many women with so much in common,
they agreed to meet every Wednesday at the same place.
With so many curls around, his roots squared up. Got excited again.
They started to grow and behave in unexpected ways.

Especially when Alice appeared between the covers
of his photon album, in a photograph of him,
on which he had written a formula for regretting
they had not slept together.

He couldn't keep his eyes off her. Mrs. Slater
tried to convince him, it was just a photograph
but the curtains parted to reveal her husband

who was so tired of him ogling his new wife,
he took a pair of scissors and 'Delilah' like
removed his head from under his hair. Curls fell to the floor.

His brain was very quickly pickled into a large jar
and placed into the waiting Electrolux in the kitchen,
which he had designed specifically for this purpose.

Later, pathologists studied it closely.
Discovered there was too much matter: not enough fissure.
Such an imbalance could cause a 'Cold Reading',
something he had been sceptical about all his life.

Yet they all readily agreed that
the relatively high number of glial cells
probably led him to take up the violin,
albeit with the wrong kind of 'Superstrings'.

AFTER READING 'CERTAYNE NOTES OF INSTRUCTION CONCERNING THE MAKING OF VERSE OR RHYME IN ENGLISH' by Sir George Gasgoigne (1575)

I bought some words the other day
but now I can't find them. They were
cheap but exactly what I wanted.
I can't quite remember what
I was going to do with them.

Perhaps there was a recipe for a poem
or an essay or perhaps it was to have
close by me, ready to use, in case a man
bothered me on the street. I remember
they were short words because

that's what I like. Monosyllabic. Like
pieces you can easily stick together.
I used to buy long words but they started
fraying at the ends if I didn't use them
by the sell-by-date and I couldn't always

find a place for them. If I fancied
making something new, I was afraid
they would be too long, fall off the edge,
look ugly. No. I seem to be doing very well
with four letter words. They come together

like the leaves of a wet plum tree holding blossom,
only letting go in moments of sweet scented fear.

'The best poetry is only a hairbreadth away from this place' – Stevie Smith

AT THE *CAFÉ SENTIMENTAL*.......

they serve tea in cups with no bottoms
to a vicar from Palmers Green.
And sometimes bottoms without tops
which is rather like Huntley's Custards
without the cream. And the drips that are seen
are quite elemental, like the heavenly liquor served
by a lattice topped tart, sweet on the vicar
and a little oriental.

The waiters wait until the end of time,
washing dirty bottoms in an essence divine.
And the eggs get broken trying to be regimental.
And the bacon gets its back up.
It's always so continental.

Sometimes there's a customer, calls herself Smith.
Sits next to the vicar, ponders the pith.
She orders rocks on the whisky
and unwinds the clocks.
He is taken aback; his collar, her socks.

She says, 'My poetry's outside but I'll not bring it in.'
He says, 'No, you're right. Let it fight to stay
alive in the alley, on the lid near the bin.'

They dance at the *Café Sentimental*
sometimes on Wednesday, if the sawdust stays dry.
And the manager is horizontal, looking for the sky in the pie.
And the vicar tells the tart to get
stuffed and not to be judgmental.

What kind of music do they play?
The kind that's left over when the piano's
passed away and the waiters are sleeping under
glasses stacked high. Waiting for that voice
from a cellar in the sky.

THE PARSNIP SEASON

Violets or parsnips
Lawrence or Beckett
A ride down a black and white avenue
Where you keep looking back
For the cat
Black and white/streaked
Or for the priest.
White and black
Doesn't matter – so long's the bible's on his back
Silhouetted words
Hide in the light
His notes, black and white
Concord your flight
Strip the paint off a kaleidoscoped night.

Parsnips or violets
Beckett or Lawrence
A trip to the cemetery
Black and white stones
Tell of multicoloured lives
Coaled bones
Under yew trees
Whose roots transfuse the zone
Blade the grass, needle this lass
Who stands with two bunches of violets
For men, I only know
Like parsnips
In black and white
Which you either love or you don't.

THE SHIRLEY VALENTINE SYNDROME

What is this thing about stones
that every other poet feels the need
to take one in their clammy hands
and try to tell us how it feels.
A grey pebble won't tell its secrets
to anyone, least of all someone
who's going to tell.
And what surprises me even more
is that it's nearly always a pebble
they go on about. Not a bit of rubble
which could be very stimulating;
it's had a lot more work experience.

I saw a man once with an old brick on tv.
He used to talk to this brick in such a way
I wanted to build a house from them.
The problem was the brick wouldn't
tell him where it came from
and of course it had no D.N.A.
But it was such a polite kind of brick
he let it lay indoors, on the table.
When friends came they noticed it
but didn't say anything. Until the brick spoke.

I've never heard a poet talking
about a brick like this which could
be wonderful. I can just imagine
them comparing its colour
with a sunset over the Colorado Valley,
its texture with the crumbling Painted Desert
and its conversation with the purling
of a stream over a pebble
on a hot canyon of a day.

RING TONES

On a giant screen, the world
witnesses a less than royal wedding
where the wind is echoing the nation's mood.

In the shop next door, an O2 salesman
is chatting up an online customer
like a double act in a silent movie.

A bit apprehensive, I step inside
as he slides off his chrome perch and waits
in the middle, a real prince charming,

surrounded by rows of mobile phones,
shining like silver bricks
walling up his fairy tale castle.

Embarassed, I hand him my old BT model
sporting an illegal plastic cover
and mumble something about a strange tone.

Its dated pattern of tiny forget-me-nots
brings a wry smile to his fake-tanned face
as he checks out the fault.

Delighted to shine in the garden
of eternal texts, he takes out his sassy,
customised model and throws me a line.

Suddenly my mobile acknowledges
his call with a cool sax rendition
of 'Candle in the Wind'.

Now in perfect working order, I head for the door
where the smell of forget-me-nots
is already dialling a long-distance number.

THE BLUES

Blue is around the edge of everything:
midnight, aquamarine, turquoise, duck egg.
It is usually seven eighths of a millimetre thick
so you can't see it. But it's there.

It comes from the ocean, holds us to the tides.
Mine sometimes increases, makes me uncertain,
pulls me in different directions but underneath
it all, it's what's holding me together.

That's why I'm mad about the Blues.
It's not because they make me sad
but they make me feel closer to things,
so close, the blue begins to shift,
starts dropping, changes to indigo.
That blue in the night, in bed alone,
which wakes me up, makes me see things
too clearly, sharply, reaching out
of a badly focused dream. It digs under

my skin, tries to get into my mind.
The fight is tough but sometimes,
just on the edge, it slips back into place
but before it does, I get a glimpse
of something unreal.

BREAD

A long time ago when I was about eleven,
somewhere in the wastes of Siberia,
a poet was sentenced to forty years

solitary confinement. All he had were sunbeams
squeezing down through an iron grill,
forming golden blocks on a stone floor.

Each day he moulded breakfast crumbs
into pieces. He played the sun,
lost the moon. Checkmated life.

A POEM I DON'T REMEMBER WRITING –
PERHAPS SOMEONE ELSE WILL!

I did not hear you breathing. You drifted
past me. A disinterested breeze caught up
in a damp cellar's dust. I saw light

through door cracks, split like the atom.
I did not feel your feet awaken
on my thighs, disturbing the last rays of sun.

Drawing in the sky, reality swept across
your eye lashed face, soft as the skin
on the first Summer's fruit. Quickly your life

awoke, spread, emptied the room. Joyful
small segments drifted and floated
weightlessly on all sides. Your hand fastened

around me slowly, as a root will hold and
collect its shaft of sun. Your foot lifts
into the straight of my back, where light must fall

all day, your toes soothe my nerves. Wildly
we become nothing, like the uneven black we saw
in the night. The sky anticipating a full arc.

COMMERCIAL BULLETIN – 1861
Guido Gezelle – Bruges– 1830–1899

Business is not doing very well in Brussels.
    What do they make there?
Carpets.

And in Antwerp, business is bad.
    What do they make there?
Paintings.

Business is not too good in Ghent.
    What is made there?
Cloth.

And in Mechelen, business is bad.
    What do they make there?
Lace.

Business is bad in Namen too.
    What do they make there?
Paving stones.

And Doornik, I hear business is bad.
    What is made there?
Mortar.

And business is bad in Hasselt.
    What do they make there?
I don't know.

In Luxemburg, business is no good.
    What do they make there?
Ministers.

But in Luik, business is booming.
    Tell me! What do they make there?
Weapons!

Translated from the Flemish by P. Suett Barbieri and published in *Acumen*

THE LAST ONE – TO THE UNKNOWN READER

Guido Gezelle – Bruges – 1830 –1899

How sweet it is to think that when I'm dead,
someone, far from here, who never knew or even saw me,
can read you, my poems, my love
and never know the sad failings of me, your father, the poet.

How happy to think that as I put my final thought down,
you will follow it along its world journey. Though troubled
and sinful as I am, there is comfort in your voice,
even some consolation.

Your voice can offer happiness, even though you wear a mask.
Your voice can heal, even though your creator is sick.
Your voice may be called even as I gasp and though tired,
support me, letting my heart open my eyes.

Oh poems! that came to me, which I have nutured
through the pain of poetry and carried in this poor heart;
poems which I have so often recast, re–clothed,
fed with my tears and moistened with my sweat,

speak for me and if God asks the reason why,
it is because you, sickly born, dragged your life
further than my gravestone and will not die, even though
I will, to prove that because of you, I dared to live.

Translated from the Flemish by P. Suett Barbieri and published by *Acumen*

WHITE

Sir Ernest Shackleton 1874 – 1922
14 Milnthorpe Road,
Eastbourne.

Beachy Head to the Polar Cap,
Some kisses linger in Birling Gap.
Discovery cracks the Antartic wake,
Scott picks ice off his fairy cake.
Shackleton's fear drops a sounding line,
trawls frosted eyes through Sussex lime.

HONEYMOON IN EASTBOURNE

Hartington Mansions
Tom & Viv Eliot
27.6.1915

Their wedding day can't settle down
to lilac rooms and quilted arms.
They drift around the turquoise streets
as blustery winds lift moon streaked palms.

Their tender love scaffolds a pier
as nervous hands twist golden clamps.
To chain the tides, staunch the fear,
the lighthouse shares its loving lamp.

NIGHT SHIFT
District General Hospital, Eastbourne

The hospital chimney puffs away
a cigarette caught in the gnarled fingers of the night.
Its soot mingles with the dark
tree lined hour, hovers, then catches
the number thirteen bus to town. It's empty.
A jogger turns a corner, gasps but clings
to the cool Avenue, determined
to avoid any white coated debate.
An African nurse, wandering home alone,
is still wearing the night.

POUND'S IN DEBT

i beseech you enter your life
Enter the dancehall of you

i beseech you learn to say 'I'
Zapateado the doubt

when I question you
Rumba in reality, make your bones anew

for you are no part but a whole
Admit no side step, partner

no portion but a being
Pally-glide into the Lustra of truth

i beseech you enter your life
Open the doors for a kyogen

learn to say 'I' when I question you
Unhinge your rampallian

you are no part but a whole
Noh, when the mask is dropped

no portion but a being
Dance in the masque of yourself

ARS POETICA

waiting ten years
for a last line.

DANCING WITH MR. ARMITAGE

Skiing must be like falling off
the end of the operating table
during an anaesthetic wondering
if you belong to this world
where pines, crows and eagles
soar through a blue passageway
ahead of you and you can't ski.
The doctor is holding your blue and white
origami dress gently in the breeze,
unfastening the ties, lifting your knee,
bending it into the wind,
taking your hand for a waltz
in the amazing theatre
of silver prostheses
where he turns and spins you
like a record on the horn box
of your childhood while you dance
to the tune of your dead mother's smile.

You wonder why people are grabbing hold
of giant matchsticks to slide down snow.
Suddenly there's a mountain of fire.
Could that be God? A flame
that flares, that makes you feel a flash
of fear between your loins,
like that was how you got here,
through a phosphorous love affair.
And where did the two sticks strike –
in a theatre, the back seat of an old car,
at a dark bus stop.

Gliding past a frozen pillow, you spin
in the ballroon of gas and glow
from heaving the swing doors
of life into the face of death.
Your knee cracks, spins and pivots,
letting you know it's on its way

to getting better. The doctor looks
at your eyelashes, strokes their sleep,
turns the keyhole of his knowledge
and allows the joint to breathe.
The snow is slippery,
you can't quite get a grip.
An eagle guides your descent
as you rent the side of a mountain
and slide back into the morning.
The beads of perspiration
on the doctor's forehead, simply
the remains of your latent snowball fight.